Arizona Watering Holes

Arizona Watering Holes

Unique Saloons & Taverns

June Stahl
and Gordon Beale

Arizona Watering Holes: Unique Saloons & Taverns

Published by Hats Off Books®
610 East Delano Street, Suite 104
Tucson, Arizona 85705 U.S.A.
www.hatsoffbooks.com

International Standard Book Number: 1-58736-520-0
Library of Congress Control Number: 2005930207

Contents

Acknowledgments

We thank all the bartenders and owners, and some patrons, for the information given to us about each saloon. This book was written on their information and stories, and we are grateful to them. Some may be truths and some may be embellished upon, but their comments and history of each saloon have made interesting stories that helped us to create this book. We thank all the owners and bartenders who gave us a pamphlet with information about their town and its past, and about the birth of its saloons.

There are so many wonderful small towns in the state of Arizona with unique saloons that we didn't have the opportunity to visit them all this time. Hopefully we will in the future.

Introduction

ARIZONA
THE 48TH STATE - 1912

Saloons were the first enterprises in mining camps and cattle towns, doing business in tents and crude wood structures until the camps grew into towns. They have always been part of the American scene—some famous and some with interesting stories. Many have preserved our history, although it was not their original intent. Many taverns and saloons have come and gone, but some adapted and remain today.

The saloons offered gambling and ladies of the evening until the advent of Prohibition closed them down. The movement toward Prohibition started years before the enactment of the Eighteenth Amendment to the Constitution. Social reformers blamed alcohol for many social ills, including poverty, health problems, and neglect by husbands. Political reformers blamed saloons for corrupting political organizations, and employers felt that drunkenness reduced workers' safety and productivity.

Many religious denominations held the position that drinking was immoral. Groups, and individuals such as Carrie Nation and her hatchet-yielding followers, emerged, raising havoc in violent saloon-wrecking crusades. The laws of Prohibition were strict, and the only way to consume alcohol legally was for medicinal purposes.

Prohibition, the "Noble Experiment," was a failure. People lost their jobs in the vineyards, the breweries, and other related industries. Organized crime came into being with bootlegging and speakeasies, amassing great wealth. The mobsters' wealth enabled them to corrupt and control police-men, the court system, and politicians. There was disrespect for the law as people illegally made home brew and wine. The speakeasies welcomed women during Prohibition. The cocktail became popular, creating a demand for fashionable drinks. With the repeal of Prohibition in 1933, taverns and saloons once again became prevalent on the American scene.

Brunswick Bars
and Back Bars

The original Brunswick bar furniture was built by special order in 1884, but the demand was so great that a dedicated manufacturing plant was set up in Dubuque, Iowa. The Brunswick bars and back bars were painstakingly hand-crafted with variations of gargoyles, lion heads, shields, and dentil moldings under the cornices. The common design of the back bar was a center mirror flanked by two smaller ones and what appeared to be solid wood supporting pillars but were wood-veneered hollow columns. The height of the front bar was for patrons, who in those days stood up at the bar, and the brass rail was essential for them to prop their boots.

Bars were made in standard length of sixteen to thirty feet with larger sizes available by special order. The furniture was manufactured in sections to accommodate the early shipping vehicles, riverboats, and wagons pulled by oxen from the East to the frontier. The Dubuque location was selected to take advantage of water transportation to freight points, and then oxen-drawn wagons were used to haul the bar furnishings. Until the railroad arrived in 1890, shipments to San Francisco were made by shipping around Cape Horn at the tip of South America. Brunswick manufactured 95 percent of all bar furniture between 1885 and 1900. These handsome bars sold for five hundred dollars then and are now fetching around fifty thousand at auctions.

In 1905, Brunswick phased out the bar manufacturing business in anticipation of the enactment of Prohibition. There are estimated to be one hundred and fifty Brunswick bars still in use. The name Brunswick is associated with bowling equipment today.

Arizona

The state of Arizona brings to mind cowboys, Indians, gold and silver mines, magnificent scenery—and old saloons that are still in business.

Arizona originally was called *Aleh-zon*, meaning "Little Spring" in Indian words. In the seventeen hundreds, the Spaniards called it Arizona. On February 24, 1863, Arizona was given separate territorial status when President Lincoln signed an act of Congress.

In 1867, Tucson was designated the official seat of the new territory. Arizona became the forty-eighth state on February 14, 1912, by an act of Congress signed by President William Howard Taft.

Copper and silver mines were discovered all over the state. Arizona is a melting pot of heritage and culture and has a lot to offer tourists. The Grand Canyon is one of the Seven Wonders of the World. It is a mile deep, 277 miles long. The famous surefooted mules offer a journey down the canyon. Visit Sedona's red rocks, Flagstaff, Oak Creek Canyon, and Lake Powell. There are twenty-seven state parks. Land belonging to Arizona's Native American tribes cover 30 percent of the state with recreational attractions such as casinos. The Heard Museum has the finest collections of native art and artifacts. To learn more of Arizona's colorful pioneer history, visit the Sharlot Hall Museum in Prescott, where documented history has been preserved.

People who like activities such as hiking, rock climbing, snow skiing, kayaking, fishing, and rafting through the wildest terrain will find it in Arizona. Arizona is blessed with sunny and warm weather. In addition, there are resorts, spas, and dude ranches that offer a Southwest experience. Frank Lloyd Wright's school of architecture, Taliesin West, is located in Arizona. Wright believed a home should coexist with its surroundings. People come from all over the country to play golf at one of the 225 golf courses. The state of Arizona is one of the fastest growing states in the country. In an hour from Phoenix one can be in a different climate. The desert in the spring is filled with a variety of colors from spectacular flowers, sand, and beautiful rock formations.

In Tombstone is the famous OK Corral and Boot Hill graveyard. In Tucson is the campus of the University of Arizona. Every town in Arizona has a unique history.

All over the state are taverns, saloons, and interesting small towns. There are historical saloons with a variety of artifacts depicting the Old West. Each tavern and saloon is unique.

The Palace Saloon

Prescott, Arizona

The Palace Saloon in Prescott is today the same impressive saloon it was more than one hundred years ago. Patrons enter through the towering massive oak doors with iron and brass fixtures into a small vestibule with an equally impressive set of swinging bar doors into the bar era. There you will find the magnificent highly polished 1880s Brunswick bar and brass foot rail. Two Winchester rifles are displayed on the ornately hand-carved back bar, offering a reminder of the saloons' participation in early justice.

Along the back wall in the large dining room is an oak-trimmed open stairway and a landing with two doors. A mannequin elegantly dressed as an early saloon gal stands on the landing, beckoning to those below. On the exquisite tin embossed ceiling remain a few bullet holes from the past.

The town of Prescott was built entirely of wood, which accounts for all the fires in its history. The Palace Saloon opened its doors in September 1877 on a dirt road known as "Whiskey Row." The official name is Montezuma Street, but it soon became known as Whiskey Row because of the many saloons. The historic Palace Saloon was one of the finest saloons and considered the grand saloon and centerpiece of Whiskey Row. It attracted cowboys, gamblers, and saloon girls. It was here that business deals were made and men came in search of work

In the late 1870s, Wyatt, Virgil and Morgan Earp, along with Doc Holliday, were patrons of the Palace. Doc Holliday was reported to have been on a winning streak of ten thousand dollars just ten months before the famous gunfight at OK Corral in Tombstone.

An upset lantern caused a fire in 1883 that destroyed most of Whiskey Row, including the Palace Saloon. The new owner rebuilt the Palace with bricks, a stone foundation, and shutters with the intent of making it fireproof. Unfortunately, the Palace was burned again in July of 1900 by another wind-driven fire that commenced its travel down Whiskey Row, consuming the wooden buildings and eventually, the Palace. This time the Palace patrons saved most of the liquor, and they saved the ornate bar by dismantling it. The patrons moved the sections of their beloved bar across the street to the courthouse yard. Legend has it that upon saving the bar, they continued to drink as the fire consumed the Palace. In 1901, the Palace was rebuilt, giving the handsome Brunswick bar a home once again.

Little Egypt was the first famous Oriental dancer in the world. She made front-page news in New York City after her infamous belly dance was raided, although she never actually stripped. In 1910, she performed at the Palace Saloon.

The American Flag with forty-eight stars (Arizona being the forty-eighth state) is still proudly displayed in the Palace.

Arizona went dry in 1919, and the Palace struggled to survive. During that time, there was a speakeasy in the basement for patrons waiting their turn in the brothel upstairs. The saloon continued to deteriorate over time until 1966, when it was restored to its original grandeur.

The saloon girls and card tables are gone, but the ghosts of the past are still lurking, and have been entertained by the various movie stars that have used the Palace in their filming. Steve McQueen starred in *Junior Bonne*, filmed at the Palace in 1971. The film *Billy Jack*, starring Tom Laughlin, had a scene in the Palace in 1971. Scenes with Peter Fonda and Brooke Shields for the movie *Wanda Nevada* were filmed at the Palace.

The Palace Saloon today is considered one of the finest saloons and restaurants in the state of Arizona. The saloon on Whiskey Row is tucked in among quaint shops, boutiques, art galleries, and Indian art.

In the historic Brunswick bar section are framed black and white pictures mounted on the wall, depicting a way of life long gone. Although the dress style has changed and there are no gun belts hanging from men's waists, the cowboy hat and boots remain popular. The spirits of miners, cowboys, and the pioneer women still seem to be roaming within the walls of the historic Palace Saloon.

Bird Cage Saloon

Prescott, Arizona

The Bird Cage Saloon was built in the 1860s on Whiskey Row and has been owned by one family, handed down from father to son. The name Bird Cage came from a family member, a taxidermist who worked with all different types of birds.

The handsome Brunswick bar features peacock feathers on top of the ornately carved back bar. Birds are definitely the theme of the saloon, which is accented by a collection of commemorative whiskey and liquor bottles with bird motifs. Everywhere you look, there are all kinds of bottles made from different designs and materials. The bar, itself, is said to have been shipped around the Cape. When it arrived, it was put into the basement of a hotel. The Brunswick bar in the basement survived the fire of 1900 and eventually was put into the Bird Cage Saloon.

Over the bar a twelve-gauge shotgun is suspended above the old brass cash register. There are also sun-bleached cattle skulls and pictures of early days on the walls.

The Brunswick bar and the large collections of birds and bottles makes the Bird Cage Saloon a unique saloon on Whiskey Row.

Lyzzard's Lounge

Prescott, Arizona

The Lyzzard's Lounge has a beautifully maintained Brunswick bar and back bar, complemented by wine cabinets, an accessory associated with luxury saloon outfits. An early picture, prominently displayed in the lounge, reflects how remarkable the bar outfit has been maintained since its original installation. Today, however, the original wine cabinets house trophies rather than spirits.

On Friday and Saturday nights it becomes a rock 'n' roll saloon. Full bands play every weekend.

Matt's Saloon

Prescott, Arizona

Matt's Saloon is a true "honky-tonk" saloon, filled with atmosphere. The saloon is one of the historical saloons upholding the old tradition of Whiskey Row.

Matt's Saloon was originally a mercantile store on Montezuma Street. The building was built in 1901 after a devastating fire destroyed Montezuma Street a year earlier. It became a saloon in the 1930s and was named after the owner.

The saloon is nestled between the famous Palace Saloon and the Hotel St. Michael. The hotel is a three-story red brick building. The architects wanted to build four stories, but that was unheard of at that time in Prescott, and the local politicians opposed them. It is said that the gargoyles, the stone faces that decorated the front of Hotel St. Michael, were unflattering images of the local politicians.

President Teddy Roosevelt and Senator Barry Goldwater stayed in the St. Michael Hotel while visiting Prescott.

The long bar is accented by a huge mounted buffalo head, deer heads, and wagon wheels above the back bar. Sun bleached cattle skulls are included in the décor, in addition to an occasional lady's undergarment suspended from the critter's horns.

Old pictures on the walls reveal stories of early years in Prescott. A few of the signed photographs of celebrity visitors are of Hank Williams, Johnny Cash, and Conway Twitty. Brooke Shields, originally from Prescott, did an autograph signing in front of the bar.

Jerome

The sketch in the early 1900s shows sulfurous smoke
from the smelters that eliminated most of the vegetation
accelerating erosion on the thirty-degree slope.

Jerome is accessible by a winding road that hugs the side of Mingus Mountain leading to the community precariously perched on Cleopatra Hill, with a magnificent fifty- mile view.

In 1876, prospectors staked the first claim. A lawyer, Eugene Jerome from New York City, was an early financial backer of the United Verde Company. Jerome never visited the town, which was named after him as a stipulation for his financial support. Copper mining at that time brought in millions of dollars.

Jerome burned three times between 1897 and 1899, causing the devastation of the town, and there was extensive rebuilding. The town incorporated in 1899, and the city officials established a building code and a volunteer fire department.

Jerome had a history of turmoil and economic ups and downs. In 1903, Jerome was known as "The Wickedest Town in the West." By 1920, Jerome had a population of 15,000, a three-shift mining operation, and thirteen hotels, twenty-four saloons, and eight houses of prostitution. People put up tents, wood shacks, saloons, and restaurants. Growth of the community was rapid, luring young men in search of steady employment and excitement, followed by gamblers, entrepreneurs, and prostitution. The only women in town were the ladies of the evening. Jerome's famous madam was

Belgium Jenny, the honky-tonk queen of the house of light love.

Around this period, open- pit mining was introduced. The sixty-six miles of tunnels beneath the community were subject to cave-ins and fires that created toxic fumes, virtually halting the mining operations. A Marion shovel used for digging the Panama Canal was brought in to assist in removing the tons of earth covering the copper deposits. The monstrous rail-mounted, revolving, coal-powered machine could move eight cubic yards of dirt in a single bite. Unfortunately, it was destroyed in 1926 when it bit into a buried dynamite charge, killing the operator and injuring several miners.

Dynamite blasting was commonly used in open pit mining, and it increased the ground movement, which was already unstable with its thirty-degree slope. It was said that any respectable tobacco-chewing man could spit from his back porch into his neighbor's chimney. In addition to the slope, there was the Verde fault, the underground spring that loosened the soil and miles of tunnels. The residents, accustomed to ground movements, accepted it as a way of life. In the early 1930s a huge blast from the mines sent the jail sliding down the hill, coming to rest one block from its original location. Some creative people referred to it as "a town on the move." Phelps Dodge now had control of the mines and following the Great Depression aggressively took advantage of the copper demand brought about by World War II. This was the last economic boom, and in 1953, with the mines shut down, Jerome became a ghost town.

The Spirit Room Saloon

Jerome, Arizona

The Conner Hotel, one of Jerome, Arizona's, oldest buildings, is home to the Spirit Room Saloon, an historic watering hole. The hotel survived the turbulent times of the copper mining town, and the Spirit Room offers a reflection of the past.

The building was constructed in 1898 and burned down shortly thereafter, along with most of the downtown area. Fortunately, it was covered by insurance, a rarity at that time, and was promptly restored. The Conner Hotel opened around the turn of the century as a bed and breakfast.

The Spirit Room has high, tin-embossed ceilings and a fashionable brass foot rail. A huge, colorful mural hangs over the back bar, showing a miner and his saloon girl, a winning poker hand, and high-stepping can-can girls in black stockings and swishing petticoats. Another mural on an adjacent wall depicts ladies of the evening beckoning miners to their balcony. Under the mural is an inscription that reads:

Ladies of The Night

Western Miners were saved from plight
By a warm smile and touch of ladies of the night
Some balance restored, men's passions freed
Like cool water in the desert, a fantasy and need

The fortunes of the Conner Hotel paralleled that of the copper mining. The hotel boomed in good times, and the building housed a newspaper, clothing store, drugstore, and a fine restaurant that was the favorite Sunday eating place for the girls of the red light district.

In the1930s during the Great Depression, the hotel closed but survived by renting the first floor space to local merchants. The population of Jerome dropped to between fifty and one hundred when the mines closed, causing it to become a true ghost town. The remaining residents focused on protecting the buildings from vandalism and decay.

In the1960s, Jerome became a haven for artists, poets, writers, and musicians. They were known as "The Hippy Generation." Through the efforts of the local residents, Jerome was officially declared a National Historic District in 1967, preserving the colorful community. Although the population is only around five hundred, Jerome still attracts over a million visitors a year.

A Journey to Crown King

The journey requires utilization of a primitive road, and for the most part, it follows an old railroad bed. Accessibility to the rich Crown King gold mines was extremely difficult because of the treacherous two-thousand-foot climbs into the mountains. The railroad was necessary to the development of the mines because of the need for heavy equipment and a method to move ore to the smelters for refining.

The road was originally an old railroad bed called "Murphy's Impossible Railroad." The railroad was completed in 1902 to bring gold ore out of the Bradshaw Mountains to the smelters. It earned its name from the treacherous route, two thousand feet up into the mountains, necessitating numerous switchbacks, bridges, and a tunnel. The switchbacks were used so the train could back up a slope and then make a run to the next grade.

Frank Murphy, an entrepreneur, was the force behind the construction of a twenty-five-mile stretch of railroad to Crown King. Naysayers scoffed at the idea, saying such a railroad would be impossible; hence, it was referred to as Murphy's Impossible Railroad.

There were cost overruns associated with the construction of five pairs of switchbacks, a tunnel, and incredibly high trestles. Crews of up to six hundred men were employed to accomplish the task, which was hampered by the severe winters of 1903 and 1904 before the railroad finally arrived in Crown King in 1904.

The railroad bed today is used as a road that zigzags up to the Bradshaw Mountains. Portions of this primitive, scenic, dirt road are carved through the rock with only one-way traffic. During the period of time between the closing of the mines and the dismantling of the railroad, residents fitted their horse- and mule-drawn wagons with railroad wheels to travel between communities. Drivers of early autos would transverse the trestles by laying down planks. The railroad was a standard gauge of 4 feet, 8.5 inches between the rails, making it a skillful maneuver to cross the bridges.

Cleator Saloon

Cleator, Arizona

Cleator Saloon is located on the dirt road leading to Crown King, Arizona. Leverett Nellis bought the land near the base of the Bradshaw Mountains and built a store, saloon, freighting business, and a cattle ranch. The name of this new community was Turkey Creek Station.

James Cleator came from the California gold mines in 1905. He invested in Turkey Creek Station. But in 1915, the partnership with Nellis was amicably dissolved with Cleator getting the town and Nellis, the cattle ranch. James Cleator changed the town from Turkey Creek Station to Cleator. However, the mines soon played out in the Bradshaw Mountains, and the railroad was dismantled in 1932. This once-vibrant community in the middle of nowhere, with only a couple of ranches and a few mining claims, became one of Arizona's many ghost towns.

In 1949, the town was put up for sale, with no interested parties. James Cleator died in 1959, and his son Tommy inherited the town. Little has changed for several decades. The general store has been closed for years, no longer selling groceries or gas. A lean-to on one side of the general store displays a sign, BAR.

Tommy operated this enterprise, in addition to his claim in the Silver Cord Mine, for a number of years. He generously shared the history of the family and the community with all who passed by the dilapidated bar, stuffed with relics of the past. Tommy died in 1971 at the age of 71, and the property is still in the family. This small saloon is operational, usually on weekends, supplying the needs of ranch hands, a few prospectors, and the occasional traveler. Time in the desert sun has weathered the crumbling buildings of Cleator, which are now only frail skeletons reflecting a symbol of a nostalgic past.

Crown King Saloon

Crown King, Arizona

At the end of this interesting journey, Crown King Saloon appears almost palatial, framed by the tall pines of the Bradshaw Mountains. The lack of accessibility has permitted preservation of the small community after the closing of the gold mines and removal of the railroad. The community's name was derived from the Crown King Mining Company that operated the largest and richest strike in the Bradshaws.

The saloon was originally in the mining community of nearby Ora Bella, and in 1916, the saloon was moved, piece by piece by pack mule over rugged terrain, to Crown King.

Tom Anderson owned the saloon for thirty-five years. Tom was a strong man and did the work of two in the mines. He was a carpenter and cabinetmaker. Tom used the building as a pool hall and a boarding house before making it into a saloon. Tom was also known as a bully who intimidated the game warden and openly served out-of-season game to his boarders. The second floor was used by the ladies of the evening. The spirit of one working gal known as Leather Belly is said to still be in residence.

The saloon survived a fire on April 1950 that consumed one house, some cabins, and a church. Twenty-two men fought the fire, saved the saloon, and then rewarded themselves by consuming a large part of the inventory.

Tom died in 1955, and his daughter sold the saloon to Grant Van Tilborg. Grant was extremely popular and a laid-back guy who could often be found relaxing on the front porch of the saloon. Anyone coming along and wanting a beer could help himself and leave the money on the cash register. Grant was a rancher but spent most of his time prospecting, his greatest passion. Many of his ore samples are displayed on the back bar. He decorated the walls with pictures of the early days and scenes from the mining communities in the Bradshaws, in addition to Crown King.

Today, the saloon is much as it has been for decades, its wooden floor worn from miners' heavy shoes and cowboy boots. In the main room is a single pool table, reflecting an earlier use of the structure, and a freestanding stove along the back wall symbolizes the warmth that was sought on cold winter evenings. There is a small stage for a band.

Some of the surrounding buildings have disappeared, through neglect, vandalism, or fire, leaving only the foundations as tombstones to remind us of their existence. The dust, at one time kicked up by horses and mules in the community, is disturbed only on weekends by pickup trucks and all-terrain vehicles attracted by events planned for the whole family. Visitors enjoy the view from the front porch with its fresh mountain air. During the week, tranquility returns to this small town among the pines.

Bisbee

Bisbee calls itself the City of Old World Charm. The city is tucked away in the Mule Mountains, not far from the Mexican border, and grabbed its share of frontier fame as a copper mining community. John Dunn, an army scout, filed the first claim in 1887. Dunn's obligation to the army prohibited him from working the claim, and he grubstaked George Warren to work the claim for him. George was not a trustworthy fellow, as Dunn found out later. When John Dunn returned, he found that George had taken advantage of the situation and had struck out on his own, ignoring John's claim. John, disgusted, sold his claim and left the area. Justice was served as George lost his claim in a wager and the claim turned out to be the most productive of the copper camps.

The town of Bisbee was named after San Francisco Judge De Witt Bisbee, an early investor who never visited the area.

His reluctance to visit the area was influenced by the continual threats of the Apache raids. Schoolchildren actually had "Indian Drills." A whistle sounded two short blasts, a long blast, and then another short blast, sending the children scurrying to the safety of the mine. It was Judge De Witt Bisbee's capital investment that led to the creation of the Copper Queen Consolidated Mining Company and changed the community from a mining camp to an industrial town.

In 1917, Phelps Dodge, through investments and buyouts, emerged as a dominant force in all copper mining activities. The demand for copper soared because of the emerging age of electricity, allowing Bisbee to enjoy a longevity not normally associated with mining towns. The town's population grew to more than thirty-five thousand and it became the cultural center of the Southwest. Despite the fineries associated with growth and culture, rough edges of society could be found in the notorious Brewery Gulch section with its forty-seven saloons and numerous brothels.

Bisbee is one more town in Arizona that reinvented itself when mining ended in the 1970s. The Victorian homes have been preserved. The town is filled with Old West history. Many film companies have used Bisbee as a background for films.

Some of the buildings still remain but no longer function as they did in earlier times. Former saloons are now quaint shops, antique shops, or galleries. Two saloons, St Elmo's and the Stock Exchange, located on the once infamous Brewery Gulch, survived and still exist today.

St. Elmo's Saloon

Bisbee, Arizona

St. Elmo's Saloon was originally located on Main Street in Bisbee in 1902. Around 1906, the saloon was moved to the location on Brewery Gulch. St. Elmo's is the oldest saloon in Bisbee, named after the patron saint of the miners. Brewery Gulch was a well-known red light district, and the second floor of the saloon was used for prostitution. St. Elmo's had the reputation of being a rough place, with numerous scuffles involving knifings and shootings. The bullet holes in the walls are testimony to many troubled days in the past.

St. Elmo's is loaded with memorabilia—handguns, rifles, swords, and knives. On the walls are posters and advertisements announcing events of earlier times. Hanging from the ceiling are a beat-up shoe once worn by an NBA superstar, an old baseball glove that appears to have been retrieved from a sandlot, and a fez that signifies the presence of fun-loving Shriners. Undoubtedly, each has an associated story. A hardy sneeze would probably create a dust storm in the saloon's smoke-saturated air.

There are indications that spiritual remnants may still remain in the saloon. A bartender shared this story: Late one evening after closing time, while accounting for the day's activity from the cash register, he heard a knock, knock, knock. Nothing irritates a bartender more than someone rapping for service after closing. He ignored the knocking. Again, knock, knock, knock. It sounded as though the knocking came from inside. He looked around, saw no one, and went on with his work. The third time, out of curiosity, he walked to the front of the room, but found no one. In the back room, a man was sweeping up, and the bartender related to him the series of events. The poor fellow's eyes grew large in terror, and he promptly fled from the saloon. He never came back—but maybe a ghost had come back.

St. Elmo's was not always a saloon. During Prohibition, the saloon was converted to an ice cream parlor, which was completely out of character for this type of an establishment. When Prohibition was recognized as a dismal failure in 1933, St. Elmo's gallantly returned to the saloon business.

The Stock Exchange

Bisbee, Arizona

In 1905, The Stock Exchange was a saloon located in the Muheim Building. This was twelve years before Arizona became a state. The saloon converted to a stock exchange in 1914 in light of the temperance movement sweeping across the country. The bar was moved to Mexico to protect it from the ax-wielding Prohibitionist Carrie Nation and her supporters, who were on a mission of destruction of consumable spirits. Unfortunately, the bar was lost when the barn it was stored in burned down.

Arizona went dry in 1919, one year before the Eighteenth Amendment to the Constitution was enacted. This had to be a devastating blow to the numerous enterprises on Brewery Gulch.

The Stock Exchange affiliated with the New York Stock Exchange, boasted a big board in the saloon that posted stock quotes, and had the distinction of having the only big board in the state of Arizona. The Stock Exchange remained active until 1961.

In 1982, it was converted back to a saloon. The bar was reconstructed, utilizing the original caged windows and counters. Today, the large board exists as part of the décor, and the original safe sits in the corner. The saloon is aptly named and reflects a segment in the history of Bisbee, first as a saloon in 1905 in the Muheim building on Brewery Gulch, and then surviving through the Prohibition era and beyond before going back to a saloon. Atmosphere and memorabilia of a stock exchange make this a unique saloon.

Tombstone

Edward Schieffelin, a prospector, wanted to do some digging. A soldier aware of the Apache warriors in the area told him, "All you'll find in those hills is your tombstone." In spite of the warning, Schieffelin set out the following year and in 1877, he discovered a rich vein of silver. He filed two claims; one he named Tombstone.

He named the town—known as "Too Tough To Die"— Tombstone. It was a town of rough men and violence. The lucrative strikes attracted card-sharks, thieves, and murderers. With the silver and gold mines at their peak, stores were opened, one hundred and ten saloons appeared, and fourteen round-the-clock gambling halls and brothels set up business. The streets were alive with all kinds of activity.

The peak population was around twenty thousand, but the mining of silver and gold had to stop because of underground water that filled the mines, making it impossible to extract the gold and silver. Tombstone then became a town of cattle ranches, with a much smaller population.

Tombstone is known for the famous O. K Corral gunfight between the Earp Brothers and Doc Holliday against the Clantons and the McLaury Gang.

Today, a re-enactment of the famous gunfight is held on most Sundays. It was this gunfight that helped make the town of Tombstone famous. Boot Hill is a cemetery of historical value, where you will find headstones of many famous villains.

Rose Tree Inn in Tombstone has the largest rose tree in the world. It is more than one hundred years old and blooms in the month of April. When you visit the town of Tombstone, you'll step back to a time that will put you in the footsteps of your great-grandparents, or beyond.

Big Nose Kate's Saloon

Tombstone, Arizona

Big Nose Kate's Saloon was built on the site of the Grand Hotel. The elegant Grand Hotel opened September 9, 1880, and offered the finest accommodations on the frontier. The bar of the Grand Hotel was in the basement, and miners came through a shaft into the basement area for some libation. The hotel handyman, "Swamper," had living quarters in the basement as part of his remuneration. The "Swamper" is claimed to have secretly tunneled into one of the mineshafts, extracted silver, and buried it somewhere on the premises. His ghost is claimed to be present in Big Nose Kate's saloon, still protecting his hidden silver.

The Grand Hotel was destroyed in the fires of 1882, but the basement bar survived and is presently in Big Nose Kate's Saloon. The bar is one of two remaining from Tombstone's heyday, the other being in the Bird Cage Theater, which is now a museum. Both bars were frequented by the Earps, Doc Holliday, Ike Clanton, and the McLaury brothers, all legendary combatants of the gunfight at the OK Corral.

Big Nose Kate spent little time in Tombstone, but her name was associated with the territory problems because of her turbulent relationship with Doc Holliday. Kate accompanied Holliday to Tombstone in 1879 to join his friend Wyatt Earp, but she soon went to the town of Globe because of her dislike for the Earps. In Globe, she bought a hotel for five hundred dollars and operated it until 1887, undoubtedly offering more than room and board to her patrons. She was reportedly in Tombstone visiting Holliday during the famous gunfight.

Big Nose Kate was born November 11,1850, in Budapest, Hungary, to a wealthy family. Many European wealthy families accompanied Maximilian to Mexico, where he was to be emperor. Kate's family then moved on to Davenport, Iowa, and unfortunately in 1865, both parents died within months of each other. Kate was placed with a guardian, and unhappy with the situation, she ran away on a steamboat. In 1874, she worked in a Wichita brothel for Bessie Earp, sister-in-law of Wyatt Earp. Kate had an ill-fated affair with Wyatt before becoming involved with Doc Holliday. She and Holliday wandered the West, building a legend of gambling, knifings, gunfights, and prostitution. After the gunfight in Tombstone and subsequent scraps with the law, Holliday was essentially on the run, and the two separated.

Kate married a blacksmith, George Cummings, in 1888. She divorced him the following year because of his heavy drinking. She worked as a maid and housekeeper for a number of years. Kate died at the age of eighty-nine, November 2, 1940, in Prescott, Arizona. Much of what she knew and experienced in her colorful life went to the grave with her.

Bird Cage Theatre

Tombstone, Arizona

The Bird Cage's name was derived from the fourteen red-velvet-draped cages suspended from the ceiling in the main casino. Ladies swinging in the cages gave the patrons an evening of entertainment. The cages inspired a songwriter, Arthur J. Lamb, to write "She's Only a Bird in a Gilded Cage," and it became one of the most popular songs of the nineteenth century.

Entertainers that performed at the Bird Cage Theatre were Eddie Foy, Lotta Crabtree, Lilly Langtry, Lola Monley, and Little Egypt. Beneath the stage was a poker game that lasted continuously for eight years, five months, and three days. It cost a thousand dollars to get into the game, and the game attracted such famous people as Adolph Busch, George Randolph, Diamond Jim Brady, and Doc Holliday. Beneath the stage were the bordello rooms. It was at the Bird Cage Theatre that Wyatt Earp met his third wife, Sadie. Prostitution was legal but did require a license and Sadie's original license is still in the theater.

The Bird Cage Theatre was the scene of numerous gunfights and knifings, in which twenty-six people lost their lives. In the walls and ceiling are one hundred and forty bullet holes, testimony to the deserved reputation of being one of the roughest, and wickedest, places in the West.

After the Bird Cage Theatre closed, it was boarded up for fifty years before it reopened for tourism. There was restoration to the exterior of the building but the inside is much the same as it was over a hundred years ago. The grand piano is in the orchestra pit, the custom-made cherry bar and back bar are still in place, and the faro tables are all still there. One of the numerous interesting artifacts is the scars of six bullet holes in the famous painting of Fatima, aka Little Egypt.

The amount of artifacts and pictures are in the hundreds that you will see on the tour through the Bird Cage Theatre.

The Crystal Palace

Tombstone, Arizona

The Crystal Palace in Tombstone was built on the site of the Golden Eagle Brewery Company. An exploding cigar caused a fire on May 26, 1882. In July of 1882, the elegant two-story building reopened, and the name was changed to the Crystal Palace. It became the showcase saloon in the fastest-growing town in the West. The second floor housed the offices of Tombstone's prominent figures, including Marshall Virgil Earp.

The fortunes of the Crystal Palace followed the closing of Tombstone's silver mining. The Crystal Palace went on a path of disrepair and was finally shut down by Prohibition. The second floor, the wooden overhang, and the wooden sidewalks were removed. The gaming tables and the famous mahogany bar were sent to Mexico for safekeeping. Unfortunately the bar was lost in a fire.

The Crystal Palace survived as a Greyhound bus station, a warehouse, and a theater before emerging as a saloon upon the repeal of Prohibition. Though back in business as a saloon, it was in a state of neglect, and in 1952 the east wall along Fifth Street collapsed.

Historic Tombstone Adventures purchased the building in 1963. This organization preserves and restores famous landmarks in the communities. Using old photographs, they replicated the mahogany bar and back bar. They replaced the wooden overhang, the wooden sidewalks, and simulated the second floor. The large round gaming table is uniquely displayed on the wall in the saloon. The colorful eagle wallpaper was chosen as symbolic of the original Golden Eagle Brewery.

If the Earps or Doc Holliday were to walk into the Palace today, the biggest difference would be the price of the drinks.

Globe, Arizona

The city of Globe is located in the magnificent Tonto National Forest. In the 1820s and 1830s, miners knew the area was rich in minerals. However, the Indians kept the miners from prospecting. General George Crook and his troops were dispatched to suppress the Indians and by spring of 1873 had the situation under control. Gold was never found, but in November of 1870 silver was discovered, with fifteen claims staked on what became the richest mine in the United States. The town of Globe was named after a globe-shaped piece of pure silver found in the area.

Globe was so lawless that miners wore pistols for protection. Robberies, lynchings, murders, and feuds lasted into the new century because if its isolation from other civilizations.

The surviving Clantons, Ike and Phineas, of the famous gunfight at OK Corral, eventually ended in Globe. A deputy sheriff killed Ike. Phineas, after serving jail time for a stage coach robbery, died and was buried in Globe in 1906

When silver saturated the market, Globe turned to copper mining, which became a very profitable enterprise and is continued to this day.

Drift Inn Saloon

Globe, Arizona

The Drift Inn Saloon was originally called the "International House." The Rabogliatti brothers built the International House in 1902. It was built of locally manufactured solid adobe bricks with decorative pressed-metal facings around the windows and cornice. The building's exterior is as it was 100 years ago. The lower level was divided into three sections, or bays, separated by cast iron columns. The six-thousand-square-foot structures at that time were the largest and finest buildings in Globe.

The saloon was a scene right out of a book of the Old West. In the middle of the floor was a trough where male patrons relieved themselves. On the south wall was a thirty-foot long bar and back bar. A loaded pistol was located every few feet along the bar for the bartender to use if things got out of line. Faro, poker, and other games were played twenty-four hours a day. An armed guard stood on a platform over the back door to oversee the activities. The madam's room was at the top of the stairs, and the ladies of the night worked in the twenty cribs along the hall. Prostitution was a successful business in the International House, but eventually local laws put the ladies out of business. It then became a boarding house and remained so until after mid-century.

The International Saloon changed hands and names several times. Since the 1980s, the saloon has been known as the Drift Inn. A feature of the saloon is the mural on the north wall, a desert scene resembling Monument Valley painted fifty years ago, but during a remodeling the mural was covered and forgotten. A few years ago, the panels began to loosen, and removal of the panels revealed the old mural. The painting was restored, and once again it is part of the Drift Inn's décor.

Cave Creek

Cave Creek got its name from a small and rare spring-fed stream that maintains a perennial flow into the area. The creek was named from an overhanging cliff over a cave. In 1863, the call, "Gold in the Bradshaws," rang out, and many miners were sure that Cave Creek would be rich in gold deposits washed down from the mountains. The feared Tonto Apache Indians still roamed the area, taking a dim view of the miner's efforts, and were an ever-present danger. The new people who arrived, brought by the lure of gold, sought federal help to assure their safety. Though the country was in the midst of the Civil War, the state of Arizona was declared a territory, and troops were dispatched from California in 1865 to establish Fort McDonald and quell their problem.

The Indian situation was no longer a threat in 1873, and a new era of mining, farming, and ranching was on its way.

William Rowe discovered gold in Gold Hill, southeast of Cave Creek, and established the Mistress Mine. In 1877, Jeriah Wood established a cattle ranch. He built his house next to the wagon road, and it was referred to as Cave Creek Station. In 1880, Andrew Jackson Hoskin took over the Cave Creek Station and cleared the land for farming.

By 1886, there were enough children to support a one-room schoolhouse. By the early 1900s, James Houck bought the Cave Creek Station and added a store. At this time, the stagecoach was in service to Phoenix and Prescott.

In 1908, a drive was established to preserve the county's natural wonder, the Tonto National Forest. The preservation regulation, unfortunately, imposed water restrictions that deprived water necessary for the ranchers and their livestock. With the departure of the ranchers, the schoolhouse was closed. The land was opened to homesteading in 1928, which successfully attracted people to the beauty of the Sonoran Desert, and the schoolhouse reopened in 1930.

During the 1920s and 1930s, people with tuberculosis came to Arizona. People believed the dry air and sun could cure them.

The Cave Creek Museum contains the history from the Hohokam Indians to the horse soldiers, from mining to ranching. Cave Creek is a fun town with many saloons, restaurants, and shops, one of the old true Western towns.

Cave Creek was incorporated in 1986. With the help of the county and state officials, the citizens were able to secure two thousand acres of the Sonoran Desert as the Spur Cross conservation area. The residents raised their property taxes to buy the land and imposed a sales tax to maintain the property.

Cave Creek citizens are referred to as genuine Cactus Huggers because of their love of the desert.

Harold's Cave Creek Coral

Cave Creek, Arizona

In 1935, Harold's opened as a small saloon on a dirt road and was known as the original "Wild West Saloon." The unique appeal was flamboyant Harold and his movie star friends that were on location in the area. Early Western actors included Gabby Hayes and Tom Mix. Later films were drawn to the location: *Rafferty and the Gold Dust Twins*, starring McKenzie Phillips, Alan Arkin, and Sally Kellerman, *Electroglide In Blue*, starring Robert Blake and Jeannie Riley, and *Little Foss and Big Halsey* with Robert Redford..

Harold's continued to expand over the years. In the saloon are two bars, one upstairs, and one downstairs.

The main upstairs bar is shaped like a horseshoe with a tree pole edging the bar. A gentlemen at the bar pointed out the marks on the pole that can be seen where the limbs were cut off. The walls in the upstairs bar are completely covered with pictures of famous people and activities from early days to the present that represents a history of the saloon.

The magnificent bar in the lower level dining area was once on a gambling boat in New Orleans. It was then taken to a hotel in San Francisco. Danny Piacquadio, owner, bought the bar at an auction and shipped it to Harold's Saloon in Cave Creek.

A sign on the front of Harold's reads: "This is Steeler Country." Harold's Steeler Club has about six hundred members. No matter where you are from on the day of a

Steeler game, you become a Steeler fan at Harold's. The parking lot is full, the fifteen TVs are on, and excitement reaches a high.

Harold's saloon contains a formal dining room with an old stone fireplace. The game room has four pool tables, video games and a pinball machine, and a dance floor.

Satisfied Frog

Cave Creek, Arizona

The original Crazy Ed's Satisfied Frog is another one of the unique saloons in Cave Creek. Crazy Ed and his wife, Maria, opened the Satisfied Frog and Restaurant in 1981. It is a wacky complex of bars, brewery, wedding chapel, restaurant, and the Goat Sucker, a sports bar with off track betting.

In 1987, Ed and Maria Chilleen came up with the idea for a brewery while visiting in Germany. Later, Ed had the idea of dropping a serrano chili pepper into each bottle of beer, and the legend was born. The peppers are pickled in a secret solution, and then each is tenderly dropped into each bottle. Their world-famous Chile Beer is sold all over the world. The Chile Beer Garden and brewery are located next to the Satisfied Frog. A slogan you may hear is "Real Cowboys Drink Chili Beer; Limes are For Wimps." After dining at the Satisfied Frog, enjoy a walk around Frontier Town and visit all the gift shops.

Horny Toad

Cave Creek, Arizona

The horny toad is an insect-eating lizard resembling a spiky-scaled frog. The name is associated with a sex-starved toad.

The previous owners named the saloon after reading this story:

The Truly Forgettable Saga of the Horny Toad

Sometime during the last century, an old prospector working the area a few miles northeast of the little town of Phoenix, Arizona, came upon a small watering hole. He thought to himself that this here was mighty purty scenery and he'd bet them Easterners would give an arm and a leg for some of this property. They could build them some roads and put up funny names on the street signs and everybody'd be carefree, even if they had to live in caves and drink from the creek. Unpacking his burro, he ate the wrapped tortilla prepared by the Mexican cook back in Phoenix before he unloaded his donkey. As he sat stirring the campfire, he noticed the ruckus the frogs were making over on the other side of the pond with their mating calls. They sure sounded anxious, he thought to himself. His aching feet reminded him not to buy any more of those two-for-five-dollar boots. As he eased the boots off to soak his tired feet, he saw the many calluses they had given him, and he said to himself, I sure am getting horny toed.

In the 1930s, Cave Creek was a rough and wild town. By the 1940s and 1950s, dude ranches and the beauty of the desert lured people to the West.

The Horny Toad was originally built in the1940s on the dirt road. In earlier times, the surrounding area had mines, caves, ranches, and a stagecoach stop. The Horny Toad has maintained its rustic structure. The original door to the saloon has a clever closer fashioned from a partially filled sand bucket that is tied to a rope strung through a series of pulleys. Additions over the years have been carefully built to match and enhance the original structure. The Horny Toad attracted many celebrities over the years, and many have lived in the area.

Wickenburg, Arizona

Henry Wickenburg, an immigrant from Germany, founded the town named for him. He was a prospector and farmer and donated or sold much of his land to the community. Wickenburg is located in the foothills of the Venture Mountains on the banks of the Hassayampa River.

The Hassayampa River moves partly underground for one hundred miles. It flows from the Bradshaw Mountains. Legend says that if you drink from the Hassayampa, you'll never tell the truth again.

The Spanish Conquistadors came first to the area, followed by the Mexicans and then the prospectors. Large-scale ranching came after the mines played out. Wickenburg also has been the dude ranch capital of the West. Known as guest ranching today, it enables people to experience what is left of the Old West.

After the mines played out, saloons and hotels were built

on Railroad Street in 1895. Those building now contain gift shops, Western wear, and jewelry stores. The antique railway station on Railroad Street houses the Chamber of Commerce, which offers information and history of Wickenburg.

Performers from all over the world perform at the Del E. Webb Center. Walking tours are available to many of the historic homes and buildings. The Desert Caballeros Western Museum is an excellent museum.

Rancho Bar 7

Wickenburg, Arizona

What makes this saloon unique is the semi-retired bartender, Wes Bodiroga, known as Uncle Wes. He has been bartending at the Rancho Bar 7 since 1942. The Anheuser Busch Company recognized him as America's oldest active bartender and presented him with a plaque that hangs above the bar. He received a "Tip of the Stetson" plaque from the Wickenburg Chamber of Commerce.

The Rancho Bar 7 opened in 1933. It was originally called Bratens Bar 7, named after seven relatives. One of the seven relatives died, and the saloon became known just as the Rancho Bar 7.

In the early days of the bar, there used to be a brass foot rail with spittoons every few feet. The brass rail is still there, but the spittoons are gone. The handsome Brunswick back bar had three massive mirrors with huge columns separating the mirrors. In the past, red lights lit up the middle mirror and the two end mirrors were illuminated with green lights. Sombreros as chandeliers flashed red and green lights onto the ceiling. The red and green lights are gone, as are the sombreros, and soft red lights now beautify the mirrors.

Illegal poker tables were once in the wine cellar; a man stood on a platform at the top of the stairs, looking through a peephole in the wall, to be able to sound a warning to the poker players of approaching police.

Uncle Wes remembered that Clark Gable once visited the saloon. A small restaurant is connected to the bar. The Rancho Bar 7 is one of the oldest saloons in Wickenburg, dating back to the time when ranchers coming into town tied their horses outside.

La Cabana Saloon

Wickenburg, Arizona

La Cabana, opened by the Pemberton family in 1945, is located across the street from the Rancho Bar 7. Early patrons recall walking back and forth between the two saloons carrying their drinks (in those early days traffic was sparse on the main road.). It was a source of wonder as to how the two saloons kept their glassware separate.

The original small bar has a glass embedded in the mirror, which is cracked. It seems the wife of the original owner got mad at him, and she threw the glass—he ducked—and it went into the mirror.

Part of the décor is an old roulette wheel, and covering the west wall is a palette knife painting depicting a Western scene. The artist painted the picture in the back room, and then traffic was delayed to carry the picture in the front door.

In 1986, two brothers, Robert and Fred Winkler, bought the saloon, which was very small with limited seating. The attached building, which had held many different enterprises over the years, became available, and the brothers bought it to enlarge their saloon. They did extensive remodeling, increasing the bar into a horseshoe configuration, adding a bandstand and a three-quarter-inch maple wood dance floor that extended into the new room, where part of the floor was covered with tile to hold two pool tables. The saloon never closed during the remodeling, and the patrons willingly helped knock out the wall. In the new bar area, there is a unique back bar with colonnades and a plaque associating it with the Sutters Mill Gold Rush of the 1800s in California. Other walls display silhouettes of cowboys, horses, and cacti, dramatized by indirect lighting. A pool tournament is held every week.

The Rancher Bar

Wickenburg, Arizona

Not far away from La Cabana, near the Hassayampa River, is Stub Hull's Rancher Bar that opened in 1978. It is a distinctive bar in Wickenburg with simulated swinging doors and images of people painted in simulated windows on the outside of the building. Originally, there were desert scenes in the window frames but Stub and an architect friend didn't care for them and decided there should be people in the frames. It's an interesting building on the outside before you even go through the doors.

In the middle of the back bar are three attractive oak cooler doors rescued from an old grocery store. Stub uses them to keep his stock cold. The bar area is decorated with cattle horns and old saddles, and the booths hold memorabilia that depicts the cowboy and rancher theme of the Old West.

When Dan Quayle owned property in Wickenburg, he and his wife used to pop into the Rancher Bar now and then. Some nights there is live music.

The Rancher Bar, with all the interesting old cowboy material, is a friendly and a favorite local watering hole.

Elks Lodge

Wickenburg, Arizona

Situated on Frontier Street in the historic district is the Elks Lodge that is home to a very interesting bar. The club members are proud of the bar and provided us with its documented history.

History of the Wickenburg Elks Bar

Con Beastrom, first Exalted Ruler, had an idea to put an old-time bar in the Lodge. He spoke to Tom Cousins, who told him about a bar in the Lion's Club in Gallup, New Mexico. The bar originally was in a saloon in Silverton, Colorado, before 1850 and was purchased by a Mr. Gurley of Gallup.

Our Elks Lodge heard they could buy the bar for five hundred dollars. The Lodge sold a life membership to Belford Howard to get the money for the bar, finances being somewhat short in the Lodge at the time.

In May 1960, Houston Anders and Con Beastrom left on a Thursday night in Mike Courtney's truck to pick up the bar for our Elks Lodge. The bar was stored forty miles north of Gallup in a tavern and was torn down and scattered all over the floor. After they got there, they had nothing to wrap it in, so they had to go back the 40 miles to Gallup to get things to wrap the bar in to keep the mirrors from breaking. This wrapping was all supposed to be done before they got there. They worked all Friday and got back in time to see Houston's daughter graduate on Friday night.

The bar was unloaded at the Lodge and was erected as it now stands.

The pillars were countersunk into the back, so if the Lodge got quarters with a higher ceiling, they could be brought up to their original height.

George Blakney raised one thousand dollars to put in the present mirrors; the original mirrors were in bad shape. The Lodge members put in countless hours removing the old varnish and refinishing it.

At a later date, Houston Anders and his son Noble drove to Phoenix to pick up some chairs and kitchen equipment given to the Lodge by Mr. Hyder.

The history of the Elks bar was supplied by Houston Anders, R.D. Jones and Tom Cousins. The reason for this history being complied was because many visiting Elks, and their ladies and guest, in admiring the bar, have asked for its history.

Charles M. Dileo
Exalted Ruler, 1971–1972

It is interesting to note that the lamps suspended over the back bar survived the Great Chicago Fire in 1871. The lamps have been carefully restored from their charred condition and donated to the club to further compliment the bar.

Pink Pony Saloon

Old Scottsdale, Arizona

You can't miss the Pink Pony prancing along the back bar. The original owner, a female with a passion for horses, named the saloon The Pink Pony in 1948. Charley and Gwen managed the Pink Pony for her. Later, when the rent was increased, the saloon was moved a block, and Charley and Gwen Brown became the new owners in 1950. The Cleveland Indians were in town for spring training and helped move the bar. Charley and Gwen's establishment became a magnet for baseball memorabilia. Charley was one of baseball's greatest fans, and the bar is a reflection of Charlie's love of the game.

One day, Don Barclay, who worked for Disney Studios, sat at the bar and began to draw caricatures of people. Charley was impressed with Don's drawings and asked him to draw his regular customers and some baseball players. Later, Gwen added some of her own caricatures of people. The caricatures are displayed all along the top of the back bar.

What is unique about this saloon is that Charlie's love for baseball manifests itself in the black baseball bats along the wall behind the bar. One side holds the bats of the American League and the other side, the National League. They are commemorative bats autographed by each team member participating in the World Series. The bats, made by Louisville Slugger and manufactured by the Hillerich & Bradsby Company, date from 1977 to 1999. In 1994, there was no

World Series because of a strike. Charley, distraught, had one light-colored bat made for each team, each engraved with the words; "Fans Are Screwed Again." No bats were made after 1999 because of the player's demand for remuneration.

An early user of the Louisville slugger was Honus Wagner, known as the "The Flying Dutchman," who played for Louisville and then Pittsburgh. In 1905, Honus Wagner became the first professional athlete to receive endorsement money by allowing his name on a product. Then, Ty Cobb, one of baseball's greatest players, signed a contract for the use of his autograph in 1905.

The clientele of the Pink Pony has included famous people: Gene Autry, the original singing cowboy owner of the California Angels in 1961; Billy Martin, the fiery often fired and rehired manager of the New York Yankees; Dizzy Dean, a Football Hall of Fame pitcher and baseball announcer known for his years with the Chicago Cubs; Harry Carry, who for fifty-three years broadcast baseball and is known for his years with the Chicago Cubs. You don't have to be a baseball fan to visit this interesting saloon and classic steak house.

The Rusty Spur

Old Town Scottsdale, Arizona

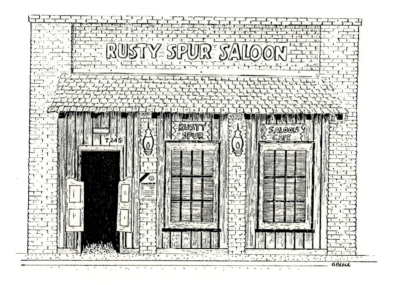

Old Town Scottsdale is a famous tourist attraction. The town takes you back into the past with its covered wooden walkways, and Western shops. People from all over the world come to Old Town Scottsdale to walk in the footsteps of cowboys and ranchers and to buy a piece of the Old West. There are a variety of shops: art galleries, Western-style gifts, Western clothing, Indian jewelry, leather, and many specialties.

The Rusty Spur is a small saloon decorated with Western memorabilia; a collection of old license plates, and dollar bills. In the middle of the room hangs a large Western wagon wheel with lights.

The Rusty Spur building is an historical landmark built in 1921. The first occupant was the Farmers State Bank. When the Depression era ended, the bank became the home of the Scottsdale Chamber of Commerce. The Rusty Spur Saloon opened its doors in 1951.

The original vault from the bank is used as a beer refrigerator behind the bar. The Parada del Sol parade is a yearly tradition of the Scottsdale Jaycees. Events include the World's Largest Horse Drawn Parade and Trail's End Celebration in Old Town Scottsdale, with gunfights. The festivities draw hundreds of people to Scottsdale and to Old Town Scottsdale.

Each year, The Hashknife Pony Express delivers first class mail from Holbrook, two hundred miles away, to the post office in Scottsdale. Riders wear authentic cowboy clothing and are sworn in as honorary mail messengers, and then they proceed to the Rusty Spur for a celebration.

Over the years, many of the Old Western saloons have seen the great men in the West. John Wayne, Ernest Borgnine, Clint Eastwood, and Jack Nicholson are a few of the celebrities who have pushed open the swinging doors of the Rusty Spur.

The Rusty Spur is a unique bar that offers memories and entertainment.

Superstition Saloon

Tortilla Flat, Arizona

Superstition Saloon and restaurant plays host to thousands of people each year in Tortilla Flat. The town of Tortilla Flat was rebuilt in 1987 after a devastating fire destroyed the previous buildings. Six residents live in and tend to the town today. Tortilla Flat is one of the last rustic towns of the Old West that reflects the fascinating history associated with the area.

Western saddles are used as bar stools in the saloon. The dollars on the walls are a long-time tradition. The local ranchers, cowboys, and men who worked on the Roosevelt Dam started the tradition of autographing dollar bills and tacking them on the wall behind the bar. Tourists picked up the idea, and there are autographed currencies from approximately seventy nations covering the walls in the bar and restaurant.

The area is rich in history, legend, and beauty. Tortilla Flat is located on the Apache Trail that was used by the Indians traveling between the central Arizona mountains to the Green River Valley. Tortilla Flat was used as a stopover by cattle drivers and prospectors lured by the gold in the Superstition Mountains. A road was constructed between 1901 and 1904 to provide access to the future site of the Roosevelt Dam. Tortilla Flat became a permanent settlement as a freight camp for supplies needed in the dam construction.

The Lost Dutchman's Mine has been a source of mystery and legend, and has inspired some of the most fascinating stories in the Southwest. The story is about two German men, both named Jacob. In 1863, one of the men, Jacob Waltz, staked his first claim. He had a thick accent and people nicknamed him the "Dutchman." The two men found a vein of extremely rich gold ore.

Jacob Waltz went to town to replenish their supplies. Jacob Wisner stayed to protect their mine. Waltz came back, only to find Wisner missing. It was assumed the Indians killed him. Jacob Waltz died on October 25, 1891, with a sack of high quality gold ore under his bed, taking the location of his mine to his grave. Many have searched for his mine, and some have died mysterious deaths in the effort.

Teddy Roosevelt passed through Tortilla when he dedicated the dam in 1911. Movie stars and notables have passed through Tortilla Flat, including Clark Gable, Glenn Ford, Ida Lupino, Alan Ladd, Loretta Young and John Wayne. Ted de Grazio, a Native American artist, and Buck Kitcheyan, Geronimo's grandson, have been guests.

Today, there are still hopeful prospectors as the legend persists, with people buying maps and making expeditions into the Superstition Mountains.

Route 66

Route 66, the most famous highway in the United States, was referred to as "Main Street America." When gold was discovered in California in 1857, Edward Fitzgerald Beale, superintendent of Indian Affairs in California, was asked to construct a road capable of supporting heavy wagons from Chicago to California. The route closely followed the Thirty-Fifth Parallel, utilizing old Indian trails. In 1925, hundreds of rural communities became part of the highway. The road in the 1930s was heavily used in the westward migration of the Dust Bowl years, and the Depression era. During World War II Route 66 supported the greatest wartime manpower movement in the history of the country. After the war, returning servicemen were lured to the warmer climate and a better life, leading to another migration to the Southwest and West.

During his second term, President Eisenhower signed into effect the National Interstate Highway System and in the 1970s, small towns on Route 66 were bypassed. The glory days ended.

John Steinbeck's classic novel, *Grapes of Wrath*, in 1939 named Route 66 the "Mother Road." Pianist, Robert William Troup, Jr. with the Tommy Dorsey band, penned the lyrics to "Get Your Kicks On Route 66." The song became popular when recorded by Nat King Cole in 1946. In the 1960s, the television series, Route 66, starring Martin Milner and George Maharis, dramatized adventures along the route. Because of a group's promotion of Route 66, people today are taking the time to get off the interstate and visit the quiet, historic highway.

OK Saloon and Roadkill Café

Seligman, Arizona

The community of Seligman developed in the 1800s when the railroad from Prescott to the main line was completed. The area was originally referred to as Prescott Junction. The town was named after the Seligman family, New York bankers with influential ties to the railroad and owners of the Hash Knife Cattle Company. Although Seligman was a rail center until the mid-seventies, it was the famed Route 66 that provided the community with its economic security.

The OK Saloon is not your typical western saloon. The frontier flavor of the region is shown on the external façade, depicting the windows of ladies of the evening. A reflection of frontier days is the covered wagon on the rooftop and the freight wagon in the parking lot.

The area is hunting country. Local hunters, and people from around the state and out of state, come here to hunt. The hunting theme is reflected in the saloon. A glass-encased room displays all types of stuffed animal. In the old bandstand are musical instruments, a silver saddle, branding irons, and an assortment of guns. A local resident with a sense of humor built the bar using a section of a seat from a two-holer outhouse.

Among the many dollar bills on the wall behind the bar you will find one autographed by June. The patio in front of the bar became the Roadkill Café.

The city of Seligman, with its tiny cottage houses on both sides of the quiet road and the vintage cars parked on the road with mannequins of famous people in them, puts a person right back into the 1930s—a wonderful experience.

The Black Cat
Saloon

Seligman, Arizona

The Black Cat Saloon has been around since shortly after Prohibition, offering libation to the local residents and to weary travelers. The building is large and square with paintings on the outside, including a large black cat.

The building is not only a saloon, but to the local residents it serves as a community center. Social events like wedding receptions, family reunions, Thanksgiving Day dinners, buffet dinners, and wakes are carried out in the large room.

Numerous works of taxidermy are on display as evidence to the skills of hunters. There has been no change in the saloon since it was built in the 1930s.

Williams

The city of Williams is recognized as the Gateway to the Grand Canyon. The town was named after Bill Williams, a trapper and mountain man in the early 1800s. At that time, fur trading was a lucrative business.

The Santa Fe line arrived in Williams in September 1882, making the town a rail center that enhanced ranching and the lumber industry. The stagecoach and buckboards began making trips to the Grand Canyon, and those trips were the beginning of the tourist industry. The Grand Canyon Railroad commenced operations in 1901 and still operates with all the engines and cars carefully restored.

Williams, like many small towns across the state, had its beginning as a rough and rowdy frontier town at the turn of the century with saloons, brothels, opium dens, and gambling houses.

In 1926, US Highway 66 reached Williams, permitting the automobile travel from the East to West. Although the interstate bypassed Williams, the town remains today a charming tourist attraction due to its proximity to the Grand Canyon.

Sultana Bar

Williams, Arizona

The Sultana Bar has the distinction of having Arizona's oldest continuous license. The bar is named after the Mississippi River steamship that exploded in 1865, killing 1238 people, including 1101 Union soldiers just released from a Southern prison. It is claimed that a family member of the original owner of the Sultana bar was lost in the fatal explosion.

Beneath the town were a series of tunnels connecting to the Sultana Bar and adjacent buildings, and a natural spring, a source of fresh water. The miners used the tunnels instead of walking through town for access to fresh water. Today, the tunnels are collapsed and the spring is now a nuisance, requiring a sump pump to keep the basement of the bar dry.

The bar survived the Depression by running a speakeasy in the basement and a soda fountain on the main floor. After Prohibition, the Sultana didn't take long to return back to a bar. Large handsome coolers, installed in the bar after reopening, are still being used today.

During the 1940s, the local sheriff was killed in the bar when he tried to apprehend a bank robber.

The Sultana Bar today supports many of the local folks' activities and games. As a tribute to a patron serving in Iraq, his shoe and a small American flag are suspended from the ceiling for safekeeping until his return.

Oatman

The town was named in honor of Olive Oatman. The Oatmans and their seven children were victims of an 1851 Indian massacre. A brother was left for dead, and two girls were kidnapped by the Indians and used for slaves. Later, the girls were sold to a Mojave chief. One daughter, Mary, died of starvation and the other daughter, Olive, was eventually found by the army and traded for a horse, beads, and a blanket. She was then reunited with her brother.

Oatman is a historic gold mining town known as a "real ghost town." In 1906, the town started as a tent camp and was located in the Black Mountains and along the historic Route 66.

After the mines played out in the 1920s, the town struggled to survive. Route 66 was officially opened in 1926, but the Arizona portion of the road was not paved until the mid-thirties, giving employment to many young men.

The massive migration following World War II provided a means of livelihood for the residents. Oatman was bypassed in the 1960s by Interstate 40 and confronted a possible extinction. Residents hung on, preserved their town, and built up the tourist trade.

The town caters to many events, one being the Laughlin River Run, which attracts forty thousand bikers. One of their favorite side trips is from Laughlin to Historic Oatman.

Oatman Hotel
and Saloon

Oatman, Arizona

The road to Oatman is a narrow, desolate, winding, twisting road, with picturesque scenery. In the small, bar dollar bills cover the walls and ceiling. Early miners and prospectors in the area started the tradition to assure them that they had one more drink coming if they went broke.

The burros are the first things you see as you enter the town. They were turned loose to run wild when the mines closed. The burros have the run of the town and don't give an inch. They roam the town searching for a pat on the head and a carrot. The burros ignore the snarling Harleys on the Laughlin run, since they were there first.

The hotel has a small saloon, restaurant, and rooms upstairs. The movie star, Clark Gable, liked to visit Oatman to get away from the hectic pace of Hollywood. When Clark Gable and Carole Lombard were married in 1939 in Kingman, due to the harassment of the press, they went to Oatman for their honeymoon. Their honeymoon suite has been retained as a tourist attraction.

William Flowers, a miner, saved enough money to send for his family. Their boat sank, and all souls were lost. Flowers began drinking heavily, and one day was found dead behind the hotel. Today, his spirit still occupies his room in the hotel.

If you want a taste of the Old West, Oatman is the place.

Payson

The community of Payson borders the largest stand of Ponderosa pines in the world. Payson originally was platted in 1882 and named Union Park. The name was changed in 1884 to honor Congressman Payson, who was instrumental in acquiring the first post office for the community.

The area's abundance of grazing land attracted cattlemen. The milling and logging industries began with the pine forest. Today, ranching, tourism, clean air, and a genial climate attract people to Payson.

The prolific writer, Zane Grey, noted for many early Western stories and the first writer millionaire in the United States, had a cottage near Payson in the 1920s. He enjoyed the fresh mountain air and the beauty of the Rim country. Here he penned the novel, *Under the Tonto Rim*.

The Payson Hotel on Main Street was built in 1932.

Main Street was the location for parades and rodeos. The Carter family once preformed on the balcony of the hotel. June Carter was just a little girl at that time.

Ox Bow Saloon

Payson, Arizona

The Ox Bow Saloon's name came from an early story of a family traveling on the trail though the area in their oxen-drawn wagon. Many months later the Army was on patrol and discovered the massacre on the trail, but the only thing they found was the ox bow. The ox bow will be part of the décor in the soon-to-be restaurant.

Payson, like many old small towns, has changed over the years due to progress, population, and fires. Fortunately, most old towns have been able to preserve a historical section. Payson's old section is Main Street.

In 1942, Jimmy Cox bought the hotel and did many improvements, constructing a motel in the back and adding a swimming pool. He carefully preserved the nostalgic and huge ponderosa pine logs and local flagstone in the structure. Jimmy Cox bought the Randall Motor Company next door and remodeled it into the Ox Bow Saloon. The saloon was incorporated into the hotel and the roof modified to give the appearance of a single building. The flamboyant Jimmy, a Phoenix resident, made numerous trips to Payson in his monoplane, landing on the dirt road and taxiing up to the front of the Ox Bow.

Jimmy had a grand opening in 1949 with many dignitaries attending. The next day, the Ox Bow had new owners—the government. There was a tax problem. The property belonged to the government until 1957 before returning to private ownership.

The present owners have spent hours extensively remodeling. The swimming pool in the outdoor patio was filled in due to leakage. The courtyard around the pool is a bandstand and is used for many outdoor events, The top of the long bar is covered with autographs of patrons, and old cowboy hats are suspended over the bar. A long bar was placed in the middle of the room with milk can seats on one side and regular seats on the other side. On the wall is a mural twenty-six feet long and eight feet high, a painting of cowboys roping cattle.

The Payson Hotel and the Ox Bow Saloon were totally different 1930s buildings, but they have successfully combined them to make one facility. The old bar and furniture built by a past owner still remain inside. The restored Ox Bow Saloon is said to represent the way it used to be in the 1950s. Until the road was improved, the entrance had been at ground level, but it is now four steps down to the door. The original doors of the hotel and the garage still exist. For more than seventy years, the Ox Bow survived many owners, the Great Depression, and neglect. From the original hotel in 1932, the Ox Bow Saloon continues to be a landmark

Charley's Pub and Grill/ Weatherford Hotel

Flagstaff, Arizona

An advanced scouting party for settlers traveling to the West came to an open field with one pine tree. The scouts stripped off the branches and placed an American Flag on the top that could be seen for miles. That is one story of many of how Flagstaff got its name—and Flagstaff was the only name the town ever had.

In 1894, Dr. Percival Lowe founded an observatory, and the famous Lowe telescope is known for the discovery of the planet Pluto in 1930.

The building that houses Charley's Pub and Grill was originally the telephone exchange office in 1910 adjacent to the hotel. In 1900, John W Weatherford, a native of Weatherford, Texas, opened the hotel. At that time, it was a magnificent hotel that attracted such guests as William Randolph Hearst, artist Thomas Moran, and writer Zane Grey, who wrote *Call of the Canyon* while in residence.

In spite of its golden past, the old downtown area became blighted with time, fires, and neglect. The historic buildings were threatened with demolition.

In 1975, Henry Taylor and Sam Green Taylor bought the decrepit buildings and began an undertaking to restore them to their original grandeur. On the third floor, the Zane Grey ballroom, with its wood floors and stained glass windows, houses the antique Brunswick bar that was brought from Tombstone. The reconstructed balcony offers a view of the historic downtown railroad district. Zane Grey's description of the hotel led Henry to discover the original fireplaces that had been covered with plaster and buried in the walls.

Charley's Pub and Grill was restored to its original façade and the décor of the telephone exchange of 1909. The Weatherford Hotel has been restored to look as it did at the turn of the century. The original hotel pub and restaurant were in the basement and are the present endeavor of the restoration process. Henry and Sam, a remarkable couple, through their restoration work have made a great and lasting contribution to the Flagstaff community.

Charley's Pub and Grill and the Weatherford Hotel ended our interesting and amazing two-year trip around the state of Arizona as we searched for unique saloons.

Printed in the United States
38512LVS00002B/67-78